My Soul Speaks
Wisdom

My Soul Speaks Wisdom

◆

A Collection of Life, Love, and Inspirational Poems for Everyday Living

Michael E. Glover

iUniverse, Inc.
New York Lincoln Shanghai

My Soul Speaks Wisdom
A Collection of Life, Love, and Inspirational Poems for Everyday Living

iUniverse books may be ordered through booksellers or by contacting:

iUniverse
2021 Pine Lake Road, Suite 100
Lincoln, NE 68512
www.iuniverse.com
1-800-Authors (1-800-288-4677)

Because of the dynamic nature of the Internet, any Web addresses or links contained in this book may have changed since publication and may no longer be valid.

The views expressed in this work are solely those of the author and do not necessarily reflect the views of the publisher, and the publisher hereby disclaims any responsibility for them.

ISBN: 978-0-595-46282-7 (pbk)
ISBN: 978-0-595-90579-9 (ebk)

Printed in the United States of America

I dedicate this book to my fraternity brother, Bryant P. Hughes, a.k.a. "B" from Washington, D.C. Bryant and I met at Johnson C. Smith University and became brothers through the musical fraternity Kappa Kappa Psi. "B" and I used to talk about becoming successful one day through all the challenges of life we faced, which is something I will never forget. Bryant saved my life, and it would not have been possible for me to be here sharing my thoughts and innermost feelings if it was not for him. I have tons of memories that will not be reproduced in this lifetime, and I will always remember the memories, kid. "B," I know you are looking down on me, and I thank you for the love and the support. If we could do it all over again, you know it would be off the hook. I wish I could have been there for you when you left this earth, but I know we will see each other again. RIP.

A Loved One Never Dies
It's what you keep in your heart
Times will be hard in the beginning
Time will progress and although
Your friend is gone,
The love and memories stay
As if your loved one
Never left.
You start to drift away;
Your mind floats off in a place
No one else can see
Nor
Feel.
It may make you laugh,
Cry,
Thinking of all the good and quality times spent.
It's definitely a good feeling.

Keep in mind—
Things happen for an unknown reason.
Keep your faith in God;
Believe in what he does.
He is not going to do anything to hurt us.
We are his children
It was written
Remember
A Loved One Never Dies.

R.I.P. to my two classmates and friends since middle school that passed and started their new life in heaven. I miss you Bill Milligan, a.k.a. "Scootie" and Maurice Jenkins, a.k.a. "Bug." One love until we meet again.

Contents

Acknowledgments

First off, I would like to thank God for life and for blessing me with the knowledge to inspire people through my poetry. To my mother Geraldine and my father Eugene, thanks for guiding and teaching me how to become a man and for being the best parents. I love you. Sherry, words can't explain how much I love you. Thank you for all the times you have been there for your little brother and for teaching me valuable lessons about life. Al, keep up the good work, and raise your kids to be successful in life brother. To a beautiful woman who has watched me climb this ladder of success and has supported me along the way: my love Mayreni. Thanks for everything. In addition, I would like to thank those who rode with me over the years throughout this wonderful journey. Also, I want to send my love to all my family and friends who reside in the Carolinas, NYC, DC, and all over the world. I am dedicating this book to you as well because all of you were such an influence in my life. Thanks to everyone who has supported my work. I really appreciate it. A big shout goes to all the poets and writers spreading words of wisdom to the masses. Keep writing, keep writing, and keep writing.

Introduction

I thank you for picking up this book. Writing has been a dream of mine because it allows me to leave reality and enter a world where it is just me. In the preliminary stages of preparing this book, I had many ideas on what I wanted to write about but just could not put it all together. I was juggling a hectic work schedule while pursuing my acting career; the time to meditate was not available. I decided to take a step back with this project. I contemplated its content and style for a few years; I finally came up with the blueprint and made a final decision. I decided to compile life, love, and inspirational poems to enlighten the minds in today's world. *My Soul Speaks Wisdom* captures all of those topics from a spiritual and emotional aspect stemming from within. I hope you will find these poems to be thought-provoking, meaningful, and inspirational. As you are about to enter my world, I would like you to keep an open mind and focus on the message presented. This compilation of poems is designed to uplift and bring awareness in hopes of encouraging you to dig deep within for self-analyzation. In addition, these poems can be used as topics of discussion to promote higher levels of thinking between young adults, adults, and folks of the older generation. Sit back and enjoy the ride. Peace and love.

M-

PART ONE:

LIFE

Life is beautiful
An experience we should be honored to have.
We do not know how long we have here
On earth;
We should live each day to the fullest
Cherish each one
Live it without regrets.
You have the power to control
Your destiny and direction.
As the days go by,
Try to look at life as a project
Strive to improve upon it.
As you constantly fix and mold yourself
Into a close-to-perfect individual,
Keep your head to the sky
Ask God for guidance.
The Almighty is powerful
And will never lead you astray.
The plan designed for our lives is
Definitely something he wants us to live out.
Also,
Find—
If you have not already discovered—
That which what makes you happy.
Life should be a great experience.

THE ROAD OF LIFE

The Road of life
Is not hard to travel.
Discouraging at times
Crossing each obstacle;
Remember your travels.
Life lessons generate knowledge;
Wisdom is acquired
At the end of the tunnel;
You will receive understanding.
The puzzle will be complete,
And it will open many doors.
Just food for thought.
Be mindful as you travel down
The Road Of Life.

SENSE OF DIRECTION

People are just living
Without a prepared agenda
Not even a goal to reach in life—
Living in the moment.
Five, ten years from now
When you look back to reflect
On what you have done,
It may be too late.
Staying on point is vital
Take some time out
Think about the path in life you want to take
Explore all options
Keep in mind—
Life passes daily and time waits for no one.
We are not promised tomorrow
Get yourself together
Write down your plans
Whatever it takes to reach your destiny,
Use your map to follow
And you will be a step closer than most
In having a
Sense of Direction.

DO NOT GET CAUGHT UP

Do Not Get Caught Up
Life has no limits.
You can do what you desire
It depends on you.
If you really want it,
Go out and claim what is yours.

Do Not Get Caught Up
When anyone tries to hold you back
Create new and better situations to work/live in
Negative energy is a hindrance.

Do Not Get Caught Up
Educate yourself thoroughly
Do not enter into a profession blind
Know what is going on
And what to expect.
The more knowledge you have,
The better prepared you will be.

Do Not Get Caught Up
Live your life.
Pay close attention to your surroundings
Even if you think
Nothing can happen to you,
Because your life is intact.

Keep in mind—
You can still slip up.
If that happens and you fall,
Get up,
Brush yourself off,
And next time
Do Not Get Caught Up

PROGRESSION IS ESSENTIAL; REGRESSION IS NOT ESSENTIAL

Progression is about moving forward in life
And making it happen.
We all have to make decisions
And
Live by them.
Take heed from past negative experiences
If not,
You will find yourself traveling down a road
Not beneficial for growth.

Progression Is Essential; Regression Is Not Essential
Do not allow yourself to be caught up with ex-mates
Who were not treating you right
When you were involved with them.
A past relationship is called a past relationship for a
    reason.
People can change and appear to be much more different
But,
Once it's over it should stay over.
Move on!
It could be the hardest thing to do
In your heart,
You know it is the right thing to do.

At the end of the day
You will feel good with the decision made.

Progression Is Essential; Regression Is Not Essential
Learn from the past
It's all about growing and grasping what has happened.
The same type of error should not occur again
Even though no one is perfect,
Going backwards, as I was taught, symbolizes
Nothing was learned.
Commit to memory as you proceed
Progression Is Essential; Regression Is Not Essential

REMEMBER

Remember
When traveling down the path to success
Make wise decisions
For the best,
Not the worse.

Remember
Love is like your favorite ice cream:
Once you have found the flavor you like,
Stick with it.
You may like others
Not all flavors are authentic or,
Most importantly,
Trustworthy.

Remember
Friends come and go
Only true ones will stand by your side
Through any circumstance.
You need to be very selective
In choosing friends.
There is a difference
Between a friend
And an associate.

Remember
You can do anything you desire to do in life
One obstacle
Between you
And
Success
Is fear.
Fear holds you back
Do not be afraid
Have courage

Remember
Faith
Overcomes anything.
A very important phrase
You have to believe
Remember

THERE IS MORE TO LIFE BESIDES FASHION AND BUTT SHAKING

There Is More to Life Besides Fashion and Butt Shaking
Do not become consumed
Or let your mind wrap around just that.
There is nothing wrong with looking nice
Wanting to shake the butt every now and then.
Do realize—
It is not going to pave the way
To future greatness.
Certain things need to be put into perspective
Value what is important for longevity and prosperity

There Is More to Life Besides Fashion and Butt Shaking
What needs to be done
In order to lead lost teenagers who are far gone?
One solution for parents:
Place more emphasis on their reading and writing.
Your child needs to grow academically,
Not learn clothing labels and the designer's name.
Mandate educational programs on television.
Your child would not have the time
To study music videos for the latest dance move.

Another solution:

Develop more community-driven activities.

There Is More to Life Besides Fashion and Butt Shaking

Take time to correct it now

It's time to reassess and reevaluate

A collective effort will bring forth change

The rest is history.

Start today, not tomorrow

Because There Is More to Life Besides Fashion and Butt Shaking.

FEED YOUR KIDS KNOWLEDGE

Feed Your Kids Knowledge.
Knowledge is the starting point
To a successful and prosperous life:
Educating our kids will pave the way for a good future.

Feed Your Kids Knowledge.
We are not living in a fantasy world;
Our kids need to keep up with society,
Not the latest rap song.

Feed Your Kids Knowledge.
Take time to speak with the youth.
Do not solely rely
On the school system
To teach them about life,
Money,
And teenage pregnancy.

Feed Your Kids Knowledge.
The future of our well-being
Lies in their hands.
Who is going to carry the torch if our kids cannot
Compete?
Encourage yourself to fight for the young ones,
Get others involved.
All for a good cause.

Spread the word and
Feed Your Kids Knowledge.

WRITTEN OFF

Quick to point fingers,
Blaming others for our own demise.
Stop with the nonsense,
Open your eyes.
The state of mind in today's society
Is get rich or die trying.
Is that what we want to instill in our youth?
The rate of incarceration
And death is rising daily.
We are all we have.
We need to,
As a people,
Get back to the days
When family beliefs—
Once the root of the households—meant something
Spend more time with your family.
It's time to stand up,
Make a change for the better
In our lives
And in our neighborhoods,
Avoid what could happen:
Being Written Off

So What Do You Think?

So What Do You Think?
Do you think people cross your path for a reason?
Is it something that naturally happens?
The older generation believes that is the case,
Just like communication is the key.
Agreeing to disagree
Breaking up to make up

So What Do You Think?
Do you believe in love at first sight?
You read and hear about it all the time.
If so,
Exactly
What is the attraction?
Vibes?

So What Do You Think?
Do you think good people are hard to find
Living on a planet where
Dislike,
Envy,
And
Dishonesty
Still exist?

So What Do You Think?
Do you think relationships today
Are more mental rather than physical?
Physical or mental?
It seems neither applies
Nowadays.
It's more like,
What can you do for me?
What kind of car do you drive?
How much money do you have?
Where is the ice?
Are those factors important?
Is being genuine and trustworthy
Becoming a thing of the past?
So What Do You Think?

WHAT HAPPENED?

What Happened?
To the traditional ways of raising our children
Discipline is a lost cause.
Nowadays,
Parents are not taking control
Like they used to.
Who is raising who?

What Happened?
To the mental state—
Teenagers growing up in today's society
Disrespecting elders
And themselves.

What Happened?
To the foundation built by two of our former leaders:
Martin Luther King, Jr.
And his I have a dream vision
What about Malcolm X?
By any means mentality …
Those men died for a cause.
They encouraged
Men and woman to stand strong.

What Happened?
To our young brothers and sisters,

Many of them are being murdered.
We need to wake up and smell the gun smoke.
If this continues,
We will destroy ourselves
And my brothers and sisters
Will no longer exist.

What Happened?
To reading the paper
And watching the news
Is becoming useless.
There are more negative stories
Than positive to report on.
This is food for thought.
Think about the words,
Written and unwritten.
Ask yourself
Or
Someone else to explain
What Happened?

PART TWO:

LOVE

Being in love is a good feeling.
When you receive true love,
Cherish the moments made.
Meeting and coming together
As one is the common goal.
At times you will not see eye to eye.
Compromising will help sustain a relationship
Along with trust.
Be understanding,
A relationship is a two-way street.
Take into account
You are not in it by yourself.
Love is love,
Love is great,
Tell the love one in your life how you feel.
If you are not in love,
Or
Being loved by someone,
Hold on
Because
Love is on the way.

WHAT IS LOVE?

What Is Love?
Ask yourself
Any answers come to mind
One seeks truth
As complex as that word is to decipher
Yet,
It is used quite often to express feelings.

What Is Love?
Could it be a combination of feelings?
What type of feelings?
How should one feel when love is involved?
Most say it is a feeling like no other
And you will know
That is the most common answer heard.

What Is Love?
Is it a thought?
A dream?
It could be a list of things.
At the same time,
We all yearn for it.
This word is used like an ordinary word;
However,
It is not.
It's a word in a class

Of its own.
Figure it out
What Is Love?

MY QUEEN TO BE

My Queen to Be
A goddess
With infinite beauty
As well as knowledge of self
Respectable woman who knows
The black man's daily struggles

My Queen to Be
Is strong and compassionate
When I am down and out,
She is my shoulder
To lean on

My Queen to Be
My daydreams are filled
With her presence
From sun up to sun down

My Queen to Be
Is not perfect
She is out there
My Queen to Be

WHENEVER

Whenever
You need to talk
My ears will listen.

Whenever
You need to release
Some tension
My fingers will massage.

Whenever
You need a hug
My arms will open up to
Console and comfort.
Sometimes,
The little things are needed.
At any given time
Morning, noon, or night.
Just to see that smile
On your face
The distance will be
Traveled
Whenever

HUGS AND KISSES

Hugs and Kisses
Represent affection.
Doing either one
Shows the receiver
What
You
Are
Thinking

Hugs and Kisses
Shared between two individuals
Having the same desire to express feelings
Through actions
Always a lovely thing

Hugs and Kisses
Very intimate
Hands moving
Up and down
Lips touching
Squeezing each other tight
Eye contact
Looks that mean something
You got to love the moments during
Hugs and Kisses

WHY SHOULD I?

Why Should I?
Believe
That you love me
When all you do
Is say the word
Day in and day out.
It's the routine
Have you forgotten?
Actions speak louder

Why Should I?
Let you into
My peaceful world.
I don't need the drama

Why Should I?
Treat you
Like my one and only
When in return
I get
Lies
And a ton of excuses from you.
Yelling
I want the person
I first met.

Why Should I?
Continue to cry for you
You stopped a long time ago.
As hard as it is living in this world,
Being with you
Does not help.
Not as close a team
Like we used to be.
Who needs the headache?
Love is not
Supposed to hurt.
I would rather be alone

Why Should I?
Give you another chance
After all of your mess.
Save that for the birds, my dear.
You want me to take you back.
Tell me:
Why Should I?

TRY AGAIN SOON

All your life
You look to the sky
And ask God
Where is my soul mate?
Times dating
Investing time
And
Energy into someone;
It does not work out.
You shy away
From getting yourself into another.
The pain and stress you felt before
Is something you are trying to avoid
And keep from happening again

Try Again Soon
Everyone is not the same—
Give the newcomer a chance.
He or she could be the one.
Try opening up
Slowly,
Though;
Take it a day at a time
See what happens
Before you focus on the present.

Let go of the past
That is yesterday's old news.
You will be ready to love again.
Give it some thought and
Try Again Soon

DO YOU REALLY MEAN IT?

Do You Really Mean It?
You will love me forever
Despite
My imperfections

Do You Really Mean It?
You will not hurt me.
Keep in mind,
You made a promise

Do You Really Mean It?
You want to have my children

Do You Really Mean It?
You say your heart belongs to me
From now
Until infinity

Do You Really Mean It?
Do not play with my emotions
I need to know
Do You Really Mean It?

DA REALNESS

When we are together,
In my spirit,
I know you are the one.
I finally discovered that mind-blowing person
Knowing I am not alone,
I feel complete again,
Especially
When you say that
I am all you ever wanted in a man.
I want you to know
You are always on my mind.
I do not want you to assume
I don't want to be with you.
It takes a lifetime to find a diamond.
Not for me
I finally found mine.
It's like a dream come true.
Outside intervention does not tempt me;
I know what I have at home.
Others do not want to see us on cloud nine
It's nothing but bitterness.
This is a blessing
Do not worry about it
It's time to be happy
All part of God's plan

How do you think we found each other?
The tissue can stay in the box
No more sad tears
Only tears of happiness
Use my shoulder
If you need to cry.
This is my seal of confirmation.
It will always remain as such
My love,
This is
Da Realness

You're on My Mind

You're on My Mind
I think about you nonstop
You make me laugh
Your company is appreciated

You're on My Mind
I feel very strong
About what we have in common
Where it could lead
A match made in heaven

You're on My Mind
Friends first,
Our friendship progressed.
Moments shared
Bliss
Memories we will always have
Continuing to build more

You're on My Mind
Daydreams of you
Making that walk down the aisle.
It's only right to let you know
The feelings are real.
Think of the long letters written

Explaining why
You're on My Mind

CAN WE?

Can We?
Unite like vintage New Edition
Live a life together
Go before God
Speak words of truth
Before the preacher says
I now pronounce you

Can We?
One day
Plant the seed of life
An image that reflects you and I
Teach him
Or her
Life is like a maze
Many directions
Options
Do not limit yourself
Explore
Encourage and support their decisions

Can We?
For the sake of our children
Expose them to traditional,
Wholesome,
Family unity.

Maintaining family togetherness is important.
Take my hand
Walk with me
The question remains:
Can We?

CURLY HAIR

Curly Hair,
Halloween night at a house party
I knew I had to have you.
I tried to make conversation
I received no response
I danced by myself with the mirror
Still,
To no avail,
I didn't stop pursuing you.
Remember when your hair caught fire?
I ran to your aid
It was my chance to have a few words with you.
Finally
Words uttered from your mouth

Curly Hair,
Our conversation was about nothing
It didn't matter to me
I was ecstatic!
The party came to an end.
If I was going to get anywhere with you,
I had to get your number.
It was all in the approach,
I guess.
Maybe you felt sorry

Or was it the orange turtleneck that persuaded you?
However,
The mission was accomplished.
I will never forget that night.
This beautiful girl captured my eyes
That was the night
I met
Curly Hair

SOUL MATE

I never knew what love was all about
Then I met you.
Feelings
Love
I felt from you
Were very authentic.
You have helped me love again
I thank you.
You came to me
When I was not looking for love.
At that moment I realized
I met love.
Expressing deep thoughts
From a past relationship
I trusted you with my heart
Daydreaming of you all the time
Thinking about a future just you and I
Kept me yearning for more.
Our first kiss was like no other
Felt little butterflies in my stomach
As I reminisce on times we shared,
The moments made,
I look forward to seeing what is next
Through the wonderful
And

Unpleasant times.
We remained tight
I can definitely say
That you are my
Soul Mate

THIS RING WILL SYMBOLIZE

This Ring Will Symbolize
Infinite love
Till death do us part
That will be the day
Imagining the reaction on your face
I love you with all my heart and
This Ring Will Symbolize

TILL DEATH DO US PART

Till Death Do Us Part
I will always love you

Till Death Do Us Part
I will always cherish you

Till Death Do Us Part
I will always make time for you

Till Death Do Us Part
I will never leave you

Till Death Do Us Part
I will always have faith in you

Till Death Do Us Part
I will always be yours

Till Death Do Us Part
I will always treat you like a queen
And I will be your king

Till Death Do Us Part
My promise
Made at the altar
Means more than anything
I hope you feel the same way I do

I love you
Till Death Do Us Part

WHEN I

When I
Say I love you
I mean every bit of it

When I
Kiss you
I want you to feel my lips
Conveying a message

When I
Hug you
I want you to feel the rush you give me
My heart steadily pounding

When I
Cuddle with you
I want you to adhere to the security
Of how my arms embrace

When I
Make love to you
Physically inclined
Is how I am trying to please.
Together mentally
Makes it even better

When I
Speak my vows at the altar
Sincerity and heartfelt words
Will flow from my mouth.
I want you to feel the love
The different forms of expression I am displaying
When I

110% PLUS

110% Plus
Giving you much love

110% Plus
Being totally loyal

110% Plus
Fulfilling your every need

110% Plus
Being very supportive

110% Plus
Dedicating my all to you

110% Plus
Always providing reassurance

110% Plus
To this marriage

110% Plus
To our family

110% Plus
To us

110% Plus
Till the day I depart this life
110% Plus

SISTER, SISTER, I FEEL GOOD ABOUT YOU

Sister, Sister, I Feel Good About You
You have what it takes to overcome obstacles

Sister, Sister, I Feel Good About You
Beautiful internally
And externally
I love your personality.
Your assertiveness and ambition
Your smile makes me come alive on hardworking days
and nights
Like caffeine

Sister, Sister, I Feel Good About You
I will give you all which is stored within
My mind
My body
And
My soul

Sister, Sister, I Feel Good About You
The one to take home to my parents
Accepted as their own
Making you feel loved
As if you were predestined to be there

Sister, Sister, I Feel Good About You
I am happy to have you by my side
Not because of what people say.
It's based on how I feel
No need to worry.
Remember,
If I am with you, I am with you.
Heartaches and breaks do not live here
Only love, this is why
Sister, Sister, I Feel Good About You

WHATEVER IT TAKES

Not sure how you are feeling
When I say this.
Absolutely faithful,
Compassionate,
And
Respectful
Satisfying your every desire
Being a complete man
To be a part of your life
All written derives from inside.
Through my actions
And
My words
You will receive confirmation

Whatever It Takes
To me,
All of this is worth it.
You are worth it
Truly,
One in a million.
I am willing to travel
That long bumpy road
Help eradicate
Unpleasant experiences from your past

Whatever It Takes
Granted a chance is given
Eye-to-eye
Has to be the plan
Communication
Without a doubt
Will be the key

Whatever It Takes
A permanent smile
On your face
Is my mission.
Let me be the one
To make it happen.
If not me,
The next man
Better step up
And
Handle it.
My only goal
Is to see you happy.
I will do
Whatever It Takes

HAVE MY CHILD

Have My Child.
I want you to be the one.
That is why you are special
And
I know
You will be the perfect mother
Of our children.
A child is a blessing
You and I combined.
One day,
I can imagine
When you come to me
Smiles galore
Shining brighter
Than the sun, moon, and stars
You saying,
"Guess what babe?
I am pregnant!"
The feeling
Excitement
Knowing that someone who may look
Or
Act like me is inside of you
Will make me the happiest man alive
Tears of joy rolling down my face

Embracing you tight in my arms
Wanting you to feel the love.
Sit down, my queen
I am not waiting until after birth
I must start right now
Kissing and rubbing your stomach
Letting our baby feel
Daddy's love.
It's confirmation to let him/her know
That I will always be there with Mommy
Like any real man should.
I will not be able to live with myself
If my son/daughter
Is living in an unjust world
Without me.
I am preparing right now
I am ready for the next step
Putting final touches
On what we created.
It will be a change for both of us
We will survive the difficulties.
I am going to take care of us
Heading this love-filled home.
I will always do what is right.
Can we start our own family?
I want to stop imagining

Will you?
Have My Child

SLEEP TIGHT

I want you to know just how I feel
The moments in your arms were amazing
I cherish every one of them
None of you taken for granted.
To set your mind at rest
Reassuring
It is all about you.
I would come to where you are
Before you go to sleep
Just to give you a kiss
Make sure you are tucked in
Leave your eyes closed
Because you would know
It is I.
A princess like you
Would recognize her prince's gentle touch.
No trek is too long.
Good night, my love
Sleep Tight

OLD SKOOL SONG POEM

Sweetheart,

At times

My actions do not speak loud enough.

Maybe these words written will

I am thinking

I CAN'T STAY.

My heart is filled with pain.

It has been like this for a minute.

This is

MY LIFE

I have to live it to the fullest.

You used to be

MY FAVORITE GIRL,

Now that is all in the past.

You were definitely

ONE IN A MILLION

I WISH

I did not feel this way.

WHEN I CLOSE MY EYES

I tend to have dreams of you

IN THE RAIN

Being with someone else.

Having such nightmares every night is scary

Thinking about that time you cheated

I am here to tell you

This
HOUSE IS NOT A HOME
Anymore.
I am not able to
SHARE MY WORLD.
FREAK-N-YOU
Is far away from my mind.
The desire to be
WICKED IN BED
Is just a phase.
I still remember
MY FIRST NIGHT WITH YOU
Was ecstasy.
From that point I said,
I WILL ALWAYS LOVE YOU.
Things changed dramatically
Sometimes,
**IT'S SO HARD TO SAY GOODBYE TO
    YESTERDAY.**
I guess that is part of life.
I am not going to continue to go
ON AND ON;
I will end by saying this
You will
ALWAYS AND FOREVER
Be my
ANGEL.

I tried to be your

SOOPAMAN LUVA;

That was not good enough.

Even though I am sad,

I still

BELIEVE I CAN FLY.

I will continue to be strong.

I hope you find that special person.

Much success to you in this life time.

I am just

RELEASING SOME TENSION.

It was something that I needed to say.

I feel like a new man right now.

I have cried

I'm not shedding anymore tears.

I hope you understand why I am leaving

I am sorry things have to end this way.

It's just an

Old Skool Song Poem

PART THREE:

INSPIRATION

In life,
We are confronted with negativity
And
Not enough positive support
To keep us focused and motivated daily.
Friends and family,
Always good for encouragement.
A role model to mimic,
The person you admire
Doing great things for themselves,
Will give you positive reinforcement
And definitely inspire you
To achieve goals and aspirations.
Keep your eyes on the prize
And
Your head to the sky.
As you proceed to satisfy your soul,
Never lose the focal point
Because of situations around you.
Everyday tell yourself
You can do it!
You will do it!
Because you want to make it!
Enjoy …

It's Up to You

It's Up to You
To maintain your mental health
Feed yourself positive food all the time
Despite what you read/hear/see.
It is on you to digest what is right and what is wrong

It's Up to You
To stick by your dreams/goals
If you don't,
Who will?
Desires to become a …
Or do …
Depend on you.
You have to put forth the effort
Goals are not accomplished
Without work

It's Up to You
You can say one thing and do the opposite.
Like I've been told and taught,
What you put in is just what you get out.
A true statement
Remember that
Decisions
The road you travel
You must overcome;

However,
There's one thing I cannot do.
That's live your life.
My friend,
It's Up to You

KEEP RUNNING

Keep Running
Fulfill your dreams
Despite obstacles that may come your way.
Continue to look at the big picture

Keep Running
Negativity is prevalent in today's time
Even from fake friends,
Friends,
And acquaintances.
They don't want to see you advance,
Only discourage you from progressing.
If you feel that vibe is in your circle,
Get rid of it.

Keep Running
Run the race with endurance
If unnecessary weight is holding you back
From reaching your career goals,
Working at a dead end job,
No promotion in sight,
Reevaluate.
Surroundings need to be corrected

Keep Running
Do not live a life

Knowing you did not finish
What you set out to do.
Achieve your every desire
The whole world is looking at you
Positive eyes as well as negative ones

Keep Running
While willing and capable
Remain optimistic,
Stay prepared,
And hold your head up.
Take these words into consideration and
Keep Running

TAKE CONTROL

Take Control
Of your life.
Be strong
Witty to sustain
Achieve your goals on a daily basis.
It is not easy.
Hard work,
Dedication,
And persistence
Pay off in the end.

Take Control
Of the driver's seat.
The direction of your vehicle
The direction you want to drive in
Everyone has decisions to make.
The ones you make affect tomorrow
Put forth a conscious effort to make ones
Wise
Thoughtful
When all's said and done,
You have to face the man in the mirror.
The person you see should be pleased with the outcome

Take Control
As you continue on the journey,

Always look to the sky for answers.
Reconfirm the plan God has in store for you
Hold on tight,
Carry on without looking back.
The road ahead is filled with potholes.
Willpower is within you to rise above
Take Control

ARMING YOURSELF WITH KNOWLEDGE

Arming Yourself with Knowledge
Being able to survive the adversities of life
Knowledge is always the answer.
Knowledge leads you to the highest heights in life.
Sign up for a library card at your local library
Take advantage of it
Check out and read plenty of books
It's free!
Never think for a second that learning only occurs
In an educational institution.
When you stop learning,
You stop growing.
Educating yourself
Should be something that you want to do.
Study,
Keep growing,
And thrive in life.
The way of keeping your head above water is by
Arming Yourself with Knowledge

BELIEVE IN YOUR ABILITIES

Believe in Your Abilities
You have the determination
And the God-given talents
To succeed in life.
Nothing will manifest
If you do not take the proper steps in securing
Your footing and direction.
As you look to lock down a plan,
Chasing your goal
Take into account
What you learned over the years.
Assess your skills accordingly
Never think that
You do not have what it takes to succeed.
Put your trust in the man above.
Everything you ever wanted to accomplish
Will manifest.
Continue to play the game
Be mindful of people
Lurking to knock you off your path
Because you are climbing the ladder of success.
Believe in yourself,
Believe in God,

And
Believe in Your Abilities

LIVE OUT YOUR DREAMS

One of the secrets of life
Is finding what you like to do
And being good at it.
It makes life worth living
Dreams motivate us to reach our potential.
They nourish our souls.
Dreams need to be fulfilled.
Do not give up!
Payoffs will be more rewarding
Than what money could do.
Money is good for living
Once the dough runs out,
What do you have to lean on?
Focus on your inner feelings
Instead of success.
Physical items will stretch thin
Dreams
Will last a lifetime.
Dreams keep you on your toes.
Living your dreams is satisfying
Start today and
Live Out Your Dreams

SUCCESS DOES NOT COME EASY

Success Does Not Come Easy
Keep in mind as you chase your goals
Success comes to those who
Consistently
Persistently
Work toward their goals daily.
Success takes time to manifest.
Being patient
Is the greatest challenge to overcome.
Without patience,
The journey may seem longer
And frustrating.
Continue to press on.
At the end of the ride,
You will reap the benefits of hard work.
Believe in self and have faith—
A life without faith will lead to problems.
The goal is to move forward, not backward
Keep these thoughts in mind
Success Does Not Come Easy

A ROLE MODEL

A Role Model
Is emulated
Influential in your life
Inspirational

A Role Model
Has the perfect swag
Without a doubt
You cannot go wrong
A perfect individual
Flawless
And definitely number one on your list
The son of God
A Role Model

DO NOT BE AFRAID TO SPEAK UP

Do Not Be Afraid to Speak Up
When you feel and
You know you have been discriminated against.
Express your concerns

Do Not Be Afraid to Speak Up
When friends in your circle head in a direction of crime
That could ultimately lead to imprisonment
Maybe even death

Do Not Be Afraid to Speak Up
If you are currently working in an environment
Where there is no respect.
Money
It's not worth being disrespected.
Have candor
Open your mouth
To rectify the problem

Do Not Be Afraid to Speak Up
If you are told to change
Your ways and beliefs,
Stick by your ethics and what you believe in.
It has to be honored

Do Not Be Afraid to Speak Up
In the world we live in,
We are confronted with politics and propaganda.
Stand for something, don't accept anything.
Your voice needs to be heard.
Make a note and
Do Not Be Afraid to Speak Up

YOU GO MY SISTER

You Go My Sister
Much success traveling down the road of life

You Go My Sister
The vision you acquired
I dig it like eating grits with cheese and wheat toast on
    the side

You Go My Sister
Achieve every desire you have
Be mindful that everything begins as a thought
Make it become reality
Incorporate it as part of your plan.
When you think you have learned everything
DO NOT STOP!
Knowledge reigns supreme.
It's stronger than any man-made key.
It will not come in your mailbox
Nor will it be hand delivered by Fed Ex at your door.
It will be like playing hide-n-seek
Not having enough clues of where to look

You Go My Sister
Conquer all goals while you are eager and competent.
I am only speaking truth
Remain in high spirits and alert

Even if the sun is not shining everyday
Keep your head up anyway.
Remember those words and
You Go My Sister

You Go My Brother

You Go My Brother
Work hard at being successful
Throw out failure

You Go My Brother
Reach for the stars
Write down your plans and implement them
While your mind is still sharp

You Go My Brother
Put forth the effort
To reach all your goals
Make it happen
In the process,
If you must cry,
Go ahead and do it.
Tears will not hurt.
Simply
Part of life

You Go My Brother
Take care of your kid(s).
You contributed 50 percent
Just as she did.
Do not brag about being a daddy;
Become a father

Raise your family
Be responsible

You Go My Brother
Learn as much as you can
Educating the mind does not cease.
Learn something new everyday
Maybe
A new word to replace curse words

You Go My Brother
Find your way
From a brother to a brother,
Keep your belief in God.
Respect all women in your life
Especially your mother.
Oust the negative
Accentuate the positive.
Without a struggle in life,
No progress will be made.
Enough said
Now
You Go My Brother

About the Author

Michael Glover was born and raised in St. Matthews, South Carolina. He received a music scholarship to Johnson C. Smith University to play the snare drum. Michael majored in history and aspired to become a teacher, but instead became an actor. He was encouraged by friends and family to pursue acting because of his comedic talent. Michael started his career in North Carolina at the John Casablancas Modeling and Career Center. In New York, he studied and completed training at The American Academy of Dramatic Arts. Michael has appeared in numerous films, TV shows, and commercials. In addition, Michael has performed in Off Off Broadway shows in New York City; one notable show was *One Flew Over the Cuckoo's Nest.*

Michael was raised by two loving parents who taught him that in order to get anywhere in life, you got to work because nothing is free. His motto is, "Giving 110 percent plus to everything I do." Michael's poetry is a reflection of life lessons received from his parents. His parents believe that repetition is the key to learning. Michael's approach to poetry mirrors his parent's teachings, as they repeatedly said, "If you say something over and over, it will stick with you forever."

Today, Michael is working in television and continues to audition. This is his first published work.

978-0-595-46282-*

0-595-46282-0

CPSIA information can be obtained
at www.ICGtesting.com
Printed in the USA
BVHW040337291220
596594BV00001BB/14

9 780595 462827